Lighten Up!

Lighten Up!

A BOOK OF ENLIGHTENED HUMOR

by Joe Sumrall

BEAR & COMPANY
PUBLISHING
SANTA FE, NEW MEXICO

LIBRARY OF CONGRESS
CATALOGING-IN-PUBLICATION DATA

Sumrall, Joe, 1960-
Lighten up! : A book of enlightened humor / by Joe Sumrall.
p. cm.
ISBN 0-939680-72-6 : $8.95
1. New Age movement — Caricatures and cartoons.
2. American wit and humor, Pictorial. I. Title.
NC1429.S816A4 1990
741.5′973 — dc20 89-48172
CIP

Text and illustrations copyright © 1990 by Joe Sumrall

All rights reserved. No part of this book may be reproduced by any means and in any form whatsoever without written permission from the publisher.

Bear & Company, Inc.
Santa Fe, NM 87504-2860

Cover illustration: Joe Sumrall
Cover & interior design: Kathleen Katz
Back cover photography: Kathleen Sumrall
Typography: Buffalo Publications
Printed in the United States of America by R.R. Donnelley

9 8 7 6 5 4 3 2 1

DEDICATION

To all of us: the Lords of the Universe.

ACKNOWLEDGMENT

"Thank you, Kathy!"

PREFACE

These animated panels are a pictorial diary, requiring very little explanation or narrative to accompany them. However, because they are as close to me as they are, perhaps a couple brief examples of how they evolved will give you a better idea of where these images came from.

The very first panel I drew was "My soulmate!" it was drawn at a time when many people around me were searching for their soulmates with lusty determination and hoping that everyone they came into contact with was a possible candidate. I would catch myself during that period asking my mate, "Do you think we're soulmates?" It seemed to be the thing to strive for at the time. As we evolve, it appears that we always answer our own questions, and so it was for me. I discovered that it wasn't important to locate, or even think about, my alleged soulmate. For the time being, then, I considered myself to be my own soulmate — until I no longer needed to look outside of myself for completion. The soulmate search seemed like a lot of energy to put out for a relationship that ultimately would be with one's Self. As I was part of that consciousness, however, it was easy for me to depict the situation in a cartoon.

The second cartoon I drew, "Patty suddenly realizes that her true soulmate is still at large," is a panel that deals with the same subject matter from a different perspective. In it, I am showcasing Patty's judgment, not her obnoxious mate amping out at a television set and his distasteful character. He is very much in his moment, doing everything in the time, place, and form he needs to. Patty doesn't seem to care for his antics any longer and has caught herself judging him for who he is. She wonders what it might be like to be with someone more compatible. Patty is at a moment when she must make a choice and maintain her power. Does she seek more harmony with the unknown destiny of her future, or does she lovingly allow her mate to reflect back to her the unconditional love she has yet to embrace? I like to think she does both.

Between these first two panels and the very last series of panels, " . . . Herman broke out . . . of structure," lie the many necessary steps and realizations that have broadened my knowledge and emotional virtue by the simple experience of them. It just so happened that my transformation began with a relationship, which, to me, was a crash course in self-discovery. Since then, watching the "Spiritual Game" and learning to break "out of structure" have allowed me personal revelations that only seem to make the experiences less describable.

There are 157 images in this book, and they all follow this heritage of thinking. If you look at them or think about them long enough, you will realize that there is a core of transformational thought behind most of them. There are other panels in this book that appear to be nothing more than cornball stunts. That's me serving you tea in a dribble cup. Every once in a while I go for the cheap laugh. These cartoons are obvious and few — so enjoy their more traditional thrust.

For the most part, these images are freeze-framed attempts to capture the profound depths of emotions with the gentleness and warmth of animation. The bulk of them represent an array of emotions I myself have passed through and dealt with. Some of those emotions have been left in the ink on the artboards as fond remembrances of wisdom gained. Others will be back — perhaps in future cartoons, but sure to appear somewhere in my reality.

As I evolve into greater knowingness, I like to think that these images are a way I can complete an understanding of my Self with the near-silent sound of a pen on paper. That sound is, for me, growing to be a more intimate experience than would be an avalanche of words — which would seek to share a feeling and, in the process, lose it.

As you peruse these rectangles of love, I trust that you will enjoy them and be able to reflect on them during the times when you, as we all do, need to "lighten up."

"GIMMICK BIN"—ASSORTED CRYSTALS AND MEDALLIONS
"BOFFING PILLOW"
"PEARLS OF WISDOM" (MUST HAVE AT LEAST 20 TO ASCEND)
"BOARD MARKERS"— (MALE, FEMALE, BOTH OR NEITHER)
The Spiritual Game
JOY! NOTHING ELSE HAPPENS HERE...
4 PEARLS
CLOUD OF DOGMA! GO BACK 4 SPACES TO REGAIN YOUR POWER!
YOU GET INTO "ZEN"... ACT HUMBLE AND VERY ESOTERIC. ADVANCE ONE
YOU JOIN A CULT, LOSE YOUR FRIENDS AND LEARN A NEW LINGO! PONDER HERE 1 TURN
YOU ACTUALLY BELIEVE A PSYCHIC READING... GO BACK 5 SPACES
YOU HAVE AN EXPERIENCE OF POWER OF SELF! IGNORE ALL PLAYERS FOR 3 TURNS
1 PEARL
3 PEARLS
2 PEARLS
"GIMMICK BIN" PICK A GIMMICK, USE AS SEPARATE MARKER AT "START" AND SPIN AGAIN!!
DOUBT!!
YOU ATTEND AN "EST" SEMINAR— FACE EACH PLAYER AND TELL THEM WHAT YOU THINK OF THEM.
YOU ATTEND A LIFESPRING SEMINAR— HIT BOFFING PILLOW AND SCREAM, "I HATE YOU MOTHER!"
"WHO AM I?"
CONTINUE IF LESS THAN 20 PEARLS & PICK "DOUBT" CARD.
INCARNATE/ ASCENSION
START/ FINISH
FULL UNDERSTANDING OF WHAT LOVE IS... IF YOU HAVE 20 OR MORE PEARLS, PREPARE TO ASCEND!
The Void ACT GODLY.
4 PEARLS
The Light ACT SAINTLY.
DARK NIGHT OF THE SOUL! WAIT HERE 3 TURNS, CONSIDER BURNING THIS GAME, CALLING A WHORE AND GETTING DRUNK.
3 PEARLS
2 PEARLS
1 PEARL
SOULMATE ENCOUNTER! WHIRLWIND ROMANCE! WHIRLWIND SEPARATION! WHIRLWIND CONFUSION!! GO TO START!
PHYSICAL & MENTAL DISCIPLINE OCCUR! FOOD AND SLEEP ARE NOW SECONDARY—GO TO "DARK NIGHT."
KNOWINGNESS.
DOUBT!
1
2
3
4
J SUMRAU

Allowing another his truth is a great exercise of wisdom.

Beginnings of an unenlightened relationship.

Patty suddenly reaches the realization that her true soulmate may still be at large.

Jerry has a profound glimpse of eternity at a rather odd moment in the men's room.

"Good!! Good Helen!! . . . You're processing anger and bitterness beautifully! . . . I'm really getting your communication here!! . . . Great communication!! . . .

"Excuse me. . . . Would you consider sharing the experience of dancing together, or do you find my physical embodiment to be a complete and total turn-off?"

How to give your power away.

Nancy struggles to integrate her feelings on men.

“Well, *of course* I know all of the powers come ‘from within.’. . . I’m only wearing these things for a little reinforcement!!”

Ivan’s obsessive need for attention grew more severe as Claire delved into her personal transformation.

"Now honey, when we connect with the isness this time, let's jump up into the pyramid and scream 'OM', O.K.?"

"They're crystals honey! . . . By wearing them during lovemaking we can expect a heightened sense of blending between our auric fields!"

Your word is law.

What you resist, persists.

Herman experiences a quantum pop in time as he suddenly finds himself turning in a test that hasn't even been passed out yet.

The graveyard gang enjoys taking a few swipes at a passing psychic.

"So where do you see yourself in the next five thousand years?"

"Damn! . . . I left my Yanni tape back at the ranch! . . . and I really need to meditate!"

Barbara experiences her very first psychic vision.

During a meditative exercise, Larry
all-too-successfully becomes one with a candle.

". . . So anyway . . . it wasn't until I realized I was chasing my tail worshipping Roger all these years that I began to look *within!* . . ."

Shelly the snail embarks on a courageous journey to discover the "unknown God."

Sidney experiences self-judgment during manifestation class.

Harold contemplates his incessant pattern of useless manifestations.

What you contemplate, you become.

Bob blows a beautiful chance of viewing self.

Ralph contemplates having prana,
instead of pizza, for lunch.

Harold practices moving molehills before moving on
to bigger things.

On the day Wilbur ascended, many clams felt that he simply jarred loose.

"They've been like this ever since I switched them from the glass bowl to the crystal one!"

Oscar returns once again as a head of lettuce to overcome his fear of being eaten.

Alan returns to defeat his racial prejudice from a past lifetime.

Bird out-of-body experience.

Out-of-body suicide pact.

Out-of-body boredom.

In a mysterious out-of-body experience, Ralph discovers the place where all missing socks go.

"So, what do you want to come back as?!..."

Old Daisy recalls a former lifetime.

"... And then I realized, IT WAS ME!! ... I was floating over the whole fish bowl, I looked down and there was MY BODY!! ... attached to me by a silver cord!! ... There was an entire universe of wonderment and beauty, then a voice saying 'GO BACK'!!"

"I'm changing, Jane ... at an alarming rate. There was a time when I looked around me here and said to myself, 'Morty, you've *made* it!' Now I don't look around that way. I look *within* and say to myself, 'Morty, you need a *drink* named after you!!'"

"Pssst!...We have more than nine lives...pass it on!"

When football players find inner peace.

MY SOULMATE!
MY SOULMATE!
MY SOULMATE!
MY SOULMATE!
MY SOULMATE!
J SUMRALL
©1989 BY JOE SUMRALL

90
THE GREAT PATH OF ENLIGHTENMENT
J SUMRALL
©1989 BY JOE SUMRALL

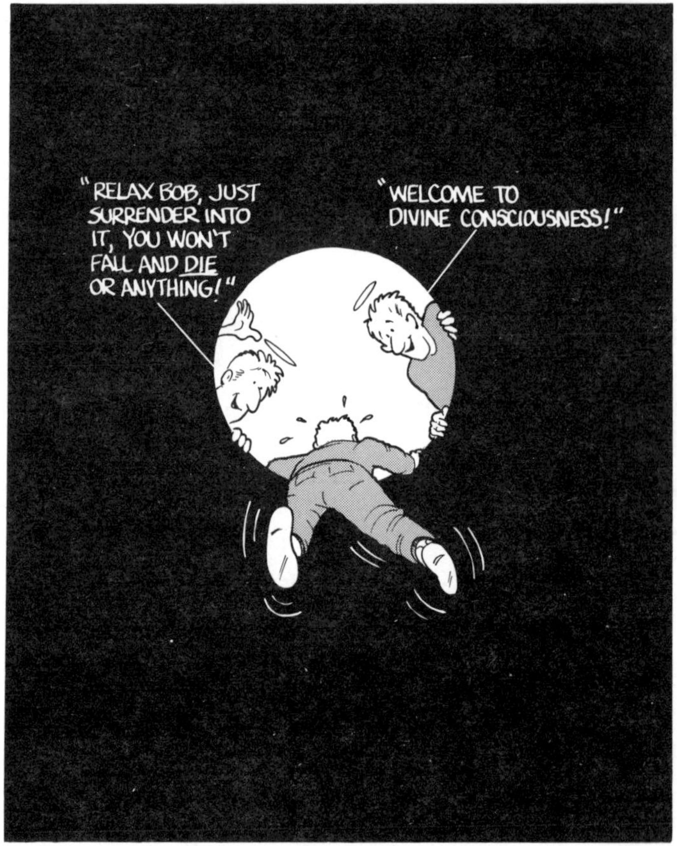
"RELAX BOB, JUST SURRENDER INTO IT, YOU WON'T FALL AND DIE OR ANYTHING!"
"WELCOME TO DIVINE CONSCIOUSNESS!"

Yogi Bear

Joe awakens.

In a supreme act of unconditional love, Bernie shows support for his wife's new vocational interests.

"Yeah, I'm stuck in traffic again, Ed . . . . Let's have the meeting in divine consciousness and my body will catch up to you guys later, OK?"

VHS HORROR
JUST KILL IT.
DEATH SINK
DEATH CHAIR
DEATH BIKE
DEATH CAR
DEATH TRAIN
DEATH BOAT
KILL, KILL, KILL
DIE, DIE, DIE
GORE ON GORE
KILLER LOVER
"AAARHG!"-
GIRL SLICER
BLOODY NIGHTIE
NIGHTMARE INN
MUSICAL SAWS
SOUNDS OF HELL
VHS HORROR
JUST EAT IT.
DEATH APPETITE
FLESH EATER
BATH OF BLOOD
BLOOD BATH
BLOOD BATH II
"OUCH!"
MURDER
CHOKE AND DIE
CHOP, CHOP, SCREAM
BLOOD BATH XXII
HOW TO KILL WELL
OPEN WOUND
LOCKED ROOM
JUST SHOOT IT.
EAT YOUR DEAD
LOVE YOURSELF
LOVE
J SUMRALL
©1989 BY JOE SUMRALL

J SUMRALL

Enlightened argument.

Another dogma is born.

BETTY?...
I SENSE THAT
YOU'RE STUFFING
EMOTION.
J SUMRALL
©1989 by Joe Sumrall

MESSIAH
ASCENSION
SCHOOL
CLASS
IN
SESSION
J SUMRALL
©1989 by Joe Sumrall

If Jesus was into image-consciousness.

Designer master wear.

Jim viewing his body as the temple of God.

To ease her self-judgment, Mildred buys a fun-house mirror.

"Twinkle, twinkle, little star, what you say is what you are."

Swami Spider

OH LOOK, THE CIRCUS IS IN TOWN.
SOMEONE CALL SECURITY...
WHAT THE..?
PERCALE... HOW INAPPROPRIATE.
BOZO.
JSUMRALL
©1989 BY JOE SUMRALL

Burt attempts to find beauty in a garden slug.

When telepathy becomes common.

Fred uses a simple visualization technique to embrace his financial reality.

Debbie receives a startling vision concerning the power of her first seal.

Bob acts swiftly as he skillfully prepares to divert another one of Al's victim stories.

What we would look like if we didn't have the part of our brain we don't use.

Through the advice of a master, Dan attempts to tell his financial troubles to a tree.

"I like this bank . . . you know what I mean? I get a real feeling of honesty from these guys!"

"The way I see it is . . . the burning trash can represents the symbol of passion within the soul. . . . As it burns through man's decadent waste, we ironically return to a simpler, more humble expression. . . . Here, my brothers and sisters, we stand as lights to the world!"

"SAVE THE TUNA!! SAVE THE TUNA!! . . . That's all I ever hear from you guys anymore! . . . WELL, NO WAY!! . . . Not this guy . . . I've lost too many buddies riding with this righteous posse!!"

Social Consciousness.

Ken gets a little testy during his first Zen 'lecture'.

Stephen spends his morning on a snowy mountain peak in silent meditative communion with the rising sun.

After carelessly walking into the wrong house expecting a surprise birthday party, Biff finally realizes he has been shot.

"ALTER EGO?! . . . You say it's my glass-blown alter ego do you!! . . . And MANIPULATOR?!! . . . Since when does an eleven o'clock curfew for your own WIFE have anything to do with a MANIPULATING ALTER EGO?!! . . .

The real reason the pyramids were built.

"Spot, I have to share something with you and you're probably going to think I'm crazy. . . . Lassie has come to me and asked for exclusive rights for the channeling use of my body; she wants to tour, conduct seminars, and sell audio and video tapes under a legal trademark!"

"I am Adweena, priestess of the jungle . . . the primordial mother of the Earth. . . . My transportation does not spew poison and beats 'bucket seats' beyond your imagination."

"Let's see now... meditation pillows, assorted crystals, Kitaro tape, pyramid poster, Ramtha videos... that oughta rack up some points with Moon Flower tonight!..."

Crystal envy.

J SUMRALL
©1989 by Joe Sumrall
PSYCHIC & PSYCHIC
KARMIC INVESTMENTS, INC.
'REAL' FORTUNES FORESEEN IN:
• STOCKS • BONDS • SECURITIES • METALS

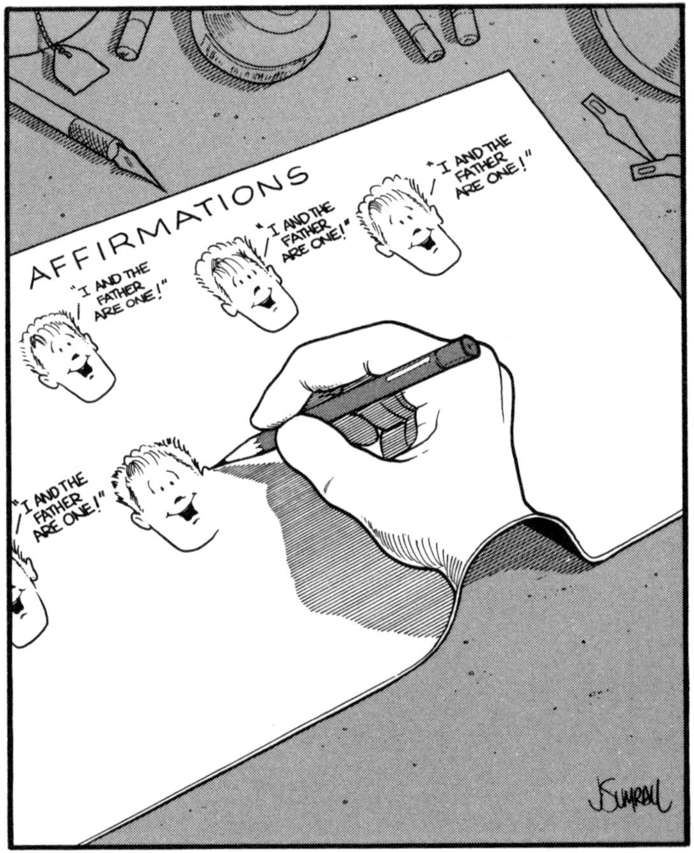
AFFIRMATIONS
"I AND THE FATHER ARE ONE!"
"I AND THE FATHER ARE ONE!"
"I AND THE FATHER ARE ONE!"
"I AND THE FATHER ARE ONE!"
J SUMRALL

How to change your aura.

Many questions arise during professor Pecan's theory of a Donovan song.

The New Age brought with it many beautiful moments of truth.

Sagittarius searches for the right pick-up line at the Astro Bar.

''Hey guys! . . . Wake up!! . . . You're not gonna *believe* this!! . . . Remember all those millions of *baby steps* we used to have to take?!! . . .''

"It's one of those new edible landscapes . . . saves me hours in the kitchen!"

Western medicine and the truthful Dr. Dork prove to be an awakening experience for Lou.

"Next!"

The three wise guys.

"Don't encourage them . . . they'll do anything for attention!"

When times are tough, gurus take the work
they can get.

Robin Hood finally engages his battle
with Victim Hood.

''The word is, we're all headin' down to Sea World and turnin' ourselves in . . . There's no place left to go! . . .''

If the solar system had human faith.

Jewish Mother Earth.

GAS & GO
ALARMIST!
DOOMS-DAYER!
FATALIST!
PARTY FART!
©1989 by Joe Sumrall

DON'T YOU SEE?!!.. AT THE RATE THE ELEPHANT IS BEING POACHED FOR THESE ITEMS, IT'S ONLY A MATTER OF TIME BEFORE THEY NO LONGER EXIST!!!....
GEE.... MAYBE I SHOULD RAISE MY PRICES....
IVORY TOWER
PURE IVORY
©1989 by Joe Sumrall

". . . No styrofoam containers for my order, son — they're detrimental to the environment!!"

Mel is hard hit when he ponders the total number of butts vs. the total number of trees.

The revenge of the rain forests.

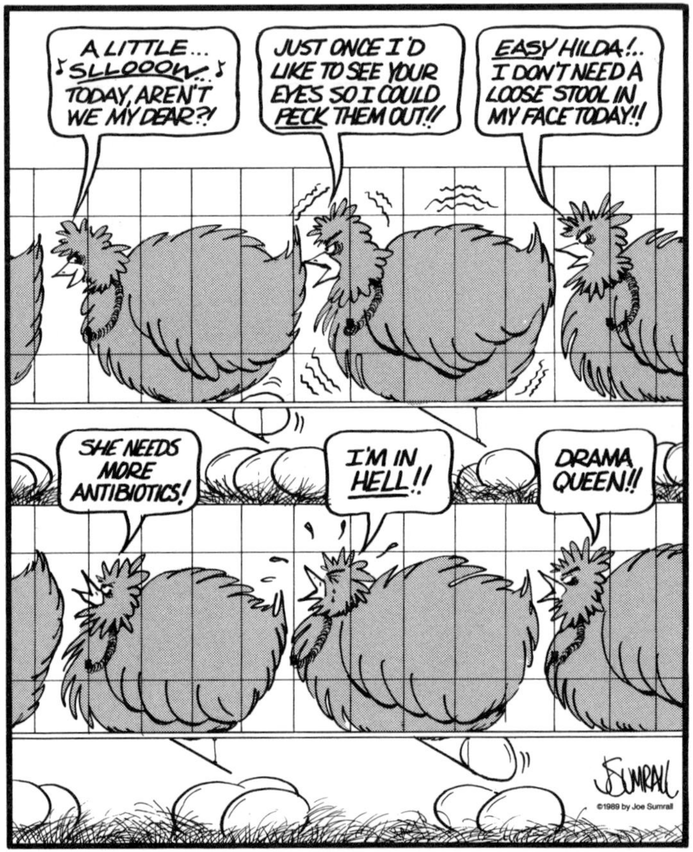

Where the term 'scrambled eggs' comes from.

Misty waivers in her commitment to the environment.

Bruce rejects his first inspiring message from his new crystal ball.

"I . . . I don't know. . . . It just shook me up, that's all. . . . I'm okay now I think. . . . God, what are we going to *do*, Barbara?"

The last man alive, in his delusion, takes one last glimpse of his own creation and *still* doesn't get it.

“You know, ascension always seemed a little far off for me in this lifetime anyway!”

Galactic intervention from the planet Noah.

The mischievous entities from the planet Hydenseak enjoy a quick game with Heather.

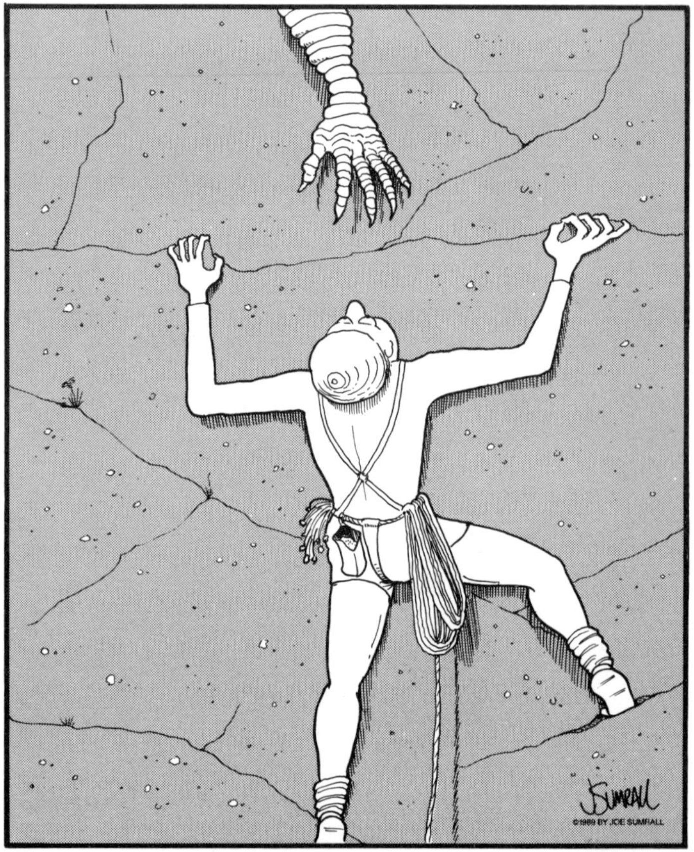

Resisting assistance from our galactic brothers is a common reaction.

"I thought you said all they did was run some simple tests while you were up in their spaceship!!!"

"Hey you guys, RELAX!... I'm only walking on rocks!! ... They're right under the water here... Stop looking so spooked!"

WOW!...
NO ONE'S GONNA
BELIEVE THIS!!...
©1989 by Joe Sumrall

"WHAT SECRETS?!...WHAT 'TREE OF KNOWLEDGE'?!... I DON'T KNOW OF ANY HIDDEN INFORMATION THAT TEACHES MAN'S DIVINITY AND IMMORTALITY!... I AM YOUR GOD, YOU ARE A HUMAN PEASANT... END OF STORY!!!... NOW, GO AND TELL THE PEOPLE WHAT I SAID... OH, AND BRING ME MY SUPPER!!"
YOU ARE GOD!
MAN GOD
MAN/GOD
BUDDHA + Y
JESUS + YO
MAN/WOMAN: GOD/GODDESS
GOD + YOU
GOD MAN IN A NUTSHELL
DIVINITY EXPLAINED
LOVE
HOW TO BE YOUR GOD
GOD
SPIRITUALITY
YOU ARE GOD

Ancient techniques of starting religions.

Unknowingly, Todd catches a light wave into another time dimension.

Why would an intelligent life form from another galaxy expose themselves publicly on Earth when we still have this as a spectator sport? . . .

When we still buy these for our children?. . .

When we still wear these?. . .

And when the movie *ET* didn't even
get one of these for "best picture"?

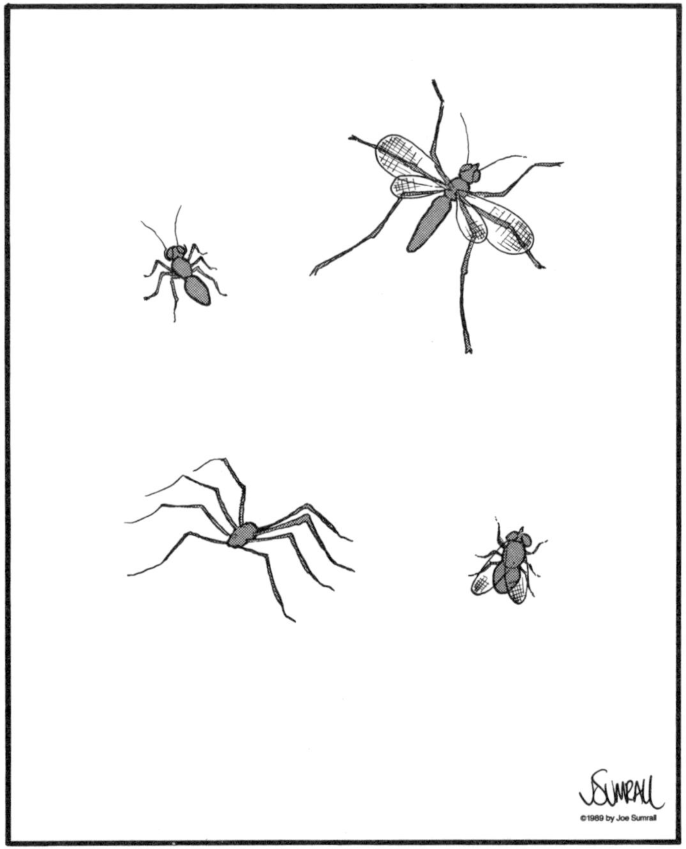

If God counted murders, we'd all be Hitlers.

"Star light, star bright, first star I see tonight . . ."

Despite Steve's lifelong dream of meeting an extraterrestrial face to face, he and his bladder lose total composure once confronted.

As historical tablets attest, ancient "gods" couldn't resist a portrait session.

Far deep in a valley of the Himalayas exist the hidden-cult worshipers of the 'Great Fallen Structure,' which channels their God, Donahue.

Sam can't seem to stay in his moment as he misses quite a show put on for him by nature.

Completely fed up with the whole "New Age" thing, billionaire Bob purchases the entire state of Consciousness.

"Don't you see?! . . . A carnivorous diet benefits neither the mind nor the body! . . . Energy becomes withdrawn, power of reasoning becomes clouded, and a sense of inertia sets in! . . ."

Sam's hearing impediment once again sheds embarrassment in his life as he enthusiastically displays his recent understanding of the teaching, "The greatest love of all is the love of shelf."

Four ways to help you sleepwalk.

"Is there a healer in the house?"

Remote-control channeling.

All statements are equally true.

If you can think it...it exists.

Mermaids

Sea Serpents

Leprechauns

Holy Mackerel

The genesis of a bad joke.

"Are you kidding? . . . I'd be *lost* without this little baby up here. . . . *Sure* it looks a little goofy, but boy when I'm at the bank, the grocery store, *wherever* . . . it just takes one quick swipe of my forehead over the scanner and *bingo*, I'm *outta* there!!"

Jane practices opening her seven seals (chakras)...

. . . Somewhere in another time flow, Luigi, Jane's unknown soulmate, rehearses the opening act of his seven seals.

When you first close your eyes and try to meditate in the God power, it looks like this.

Then it starts looking like this.

Then, after a while, it looks like this again.

Finally, with passion and practice, it looks something like this.

If every little star,

Every speck of sand,

And every hair on our heads
is known to the isness,

Then do you suppose
it's counting our trash?

Movie Mongers.

War Mongers.

YIELD
JSUMRALL

JSUMRALL

Some watched with exhilaration,

some watched with fear,

as Herman broke out of structure.

ABOUT THE AUTHOR

Joe Sumrall received his art education at Art Center College of Design in Pasadena, California. He owned and creatively operated Sumrall Chu & Associates, a very successful advertising agency in Newport Beach, California, for seven years before he gave the agency away and moved to western Washington state in 1987.

Realizing that advertising was counterproductive to his sense of direction, Sumrall felt the need to engage his abilities in a goal that was as stimulating for him as was his desire to contribute to the evolution of consciousness. Having seen his advertising work appear in innumerable locations and forms, from newspapers to annual reports, he began creating his animated panels to fulfill his need to communicate a higher frequency series of thoughts. His images have since appeared in numerous national publications, including *East West, Body Mind & Spirit, The Quest, Windwords,* and *The Monthly Aspectarian*.

Sumrall is currently developing new animated creations for his second book, *Wake Up!*, and is actively involved as a creative consultant and graphic designer for an advertising agency in southern California. He continually engages new understandings with his numerous exposures to enlightened schools of thought. He is also a devout avatar and immortalist.

BOOKS OF RELATED INTEREST
BY BEAR & COMPANY

THE EMERGING NEW AGE
by J.L. Simmons

SURFERS OF THE ZUVUYA
Tales of Interdimensional Travel
by José Argüelles

Contact your local bookseller or write:
BEAR & COMPANY
P.O. Drawer 2860
Santa Fe, NM 87504